# Midnight Milkshakes

## Ice Cream And Suicide Vol. II

By Jack Ray

"A mighty flame follows a tiny spark."
-Dante Alighieri

## Down The Rabbit Hole

And it's with those poems I seduced you
Lured you in to me
You couldn't believe
Anyone would feel that much for you
That anyone could say the things I said about you
How enchanting you were
How hypnotic
But now without you
It's with these poems I lay you to rest for good
In a grave marked

*Wash away, never look back, erased from my mind.*

## The Night We Met

We glowed so brilliantly together
A flame that would never die
In absence we barely flickered
Us fireflies in a jar
Released from one another
Becoming nothing
But lonesome sparks in the night.

**Head And Shoulders**

And there were plenty of times
My love for you was visible on my face
Especially when I'd talk about everything
You could do to rule the world
With nothing but a smile.

## Midnight Milkshakes

I found peace
In spending Friday nights alone with you
Sipping milkshakes at midnight
Us dreaming about the future
Visions in each other's eyes
With one look you always knew how to get me
What I wouldn't give to relive that one last time.

## We Need To Talk

We sat across each other that night
Snow fell outside our window
And our fates became intertwined when you said
    You wanted more
You didn't want to settle for the treatment
    Your man was giving you
You wanted to be a priority
You wanted to be loved
And from that night we built our homes
    In each other's hearts
I found the greatest life possible in you
We were happy for the first time
But for some reason
    You couldn't wipe the guilt from your hands
The guilt of us
So you let me fall
    Rather than live with your decisions
You built me up
You lead me on
Not knowing how much it bothered you
    Until you couldn't take the heat any longer
So you sent me to the Furnace in your place
    Without any warning
And in the fire I'll burn for you *always*.

**Those Three Words**

We would spend our mornings in the coffee shop
Two iced and a blueberry muffin for the lady
We'd watch the people and laugh in secret
We'd locked our eyes like we met for the first time
And I was lucky enough to get this every morning
I wish you knew
     How badly I felt it then
I wish you knew
     How much you made my every day
Over and over again
I wish you knew
     Before you let it slip away.

## Victorian Era Homes

There is a time I often think about
We would walk
    The cold autumn sidewalks together
And I was balancing the ideas in my head
Whether I truly loved you and wanted you in
Or whether I was a fool
    To be played by a taken women
And I was a fool you see
Because I didn't want to believe it
I wanted you and your love
And there was simply never anything else
This world could have tried to stop me
But it would have been in vain
I was blinded by you
And I did fall for you...
Not realizing that this fall would be something
    I'd never recover from.

## You Really Are A Hopeless Romantic

Back when you lied to him
Ignoring his calls
Feeling that bitterness in your heart toward him
*WE  BURNED  BRIGHT*
You took my hand and showed me
            The possibilities of a world
                        In love
                                    With you
And I desperately needed that place
The only dream worth dreaming
And after fighting with all that I am
We turned that fantasy into reality
…But you slowly began to lie to me too
            Over nothing
You doused the flame
You hated me for coming into your life
            The way I did
But I still loved you
I still believed you when you said
            You wanted it too before it collapsed,
In the end I still gave you reassurance of my love
I was still affectionate to you
            But you were cold then
You couldn't even pretend to miss me
Pretend to care at all
You were numb to me
            Even after everything.

**University 101**

What happened to us?
You used to hug me tight after a long day
And I would always whisper to you
        How much I never wanted you to let go.

## This Family Dynamic

The night we met
How long ago
We seemed so perfect
You were my half
     Identical, in nearly every way
But as time passed
My infatuation grew into love
While you stared blank
     And you kept staring
          Hollowed on the inside
But making me believe we were still in love
You were like me after all
     Identical, in almost every way
Well so I thought,
Until you woke me up in the middle of the night
     To let me know it was over
     To let me know you never loved me
     To tell me to forget and move on
I never felt this…so how could you?
I thought we were cut from the same cloth
How could you forget?
     Change?
          What happened?
          And what did I do wrong?
Questions I'll never know the answers to
Along with any other lies, hidden,
     That made me believe
          You were just like me.

**Mama And Papa**

You were my world
My lover
And my best friend
Now I'm not even allowed to utter your name.

## I Like You A Pretty Decent Amount

The warmth of your body next to me
I'll never know that comfort again
To think we really had something special
To be so foolish to fall for you
        It haunts me
        It haunts me when I walk alone
        It haunts me when I dine, alone
But I think the most painful experience
        It's seeing you across the room
And me trying so desperately to catch a glimpse
I try to fight you
But every now and then I'll look to you
Hoping to God that you are fighting it too
That you want to catch a glimpse too
And that our eyes will meet and say;
        *I'm sorry*
        *I miss you*
        Or even a fucking *hello*
No, you see
That shit doesn't happen
I look to you
        And you don't move a muscle
            Stone cold
It's as if you hate me for something
And I don't know what
        All I ever did was love you
But you, you act like I'm a dead man walking.

**Immaturity // Frosty**

You were so thankful to have me in your life
You struggled to imagine
          A day going by without me
But somehow, someway
You were still the one to get rid of me.

## 10 Gallon

In the comfort of our home
We'd watch the fish chase
Playfully they ran around the tank
And deep down we knew they loved each other
After all, they were the only company they had

Funny how similar we were
How I always chased you
How we ran around for what seemed like
        A lifetime
But you knew I loved you from the beginning
You were my company and I was yours
        But you left me
You've swam far from me without explanation
Yet I still chase your ghost
Still reliving that memory of you
        That love for you
And in circles I'll run
        Trying to get you back
        Trying to understand
        Trying to find that lover who ran circles
                In my heart.

**Sent From**

'You made my life better'
Something you said as you shattered my heart
Obviously not true
Obviously not good enough
      Maybe I just wasn't
And that was something I worried about
      Since even before we took the leap
You told me not to worry about it
That I was in fact 'better than the rest'
So why leave me
Why make such a bold remark as
      'You made my life better'
        If I truly didn't
How could you, with a press of a button,
      Turn my life into a living hell.

## Malebolge

You wanted it as much as I did
To give into that evil desire
To feel our bodies so close and so hot
To take the plunge into something sinister
And while you made out with pleasure
You painted me in blame.

## I Feel Different Now

And in the last moment we shared
I told you I loved you
And in the last moment we shared
You reminded me you never did

And in this moment
I still dream of loving you
And in this moment
You remember you never could.

**Studying Chemistry**

And I stop to relive it every time
Those desires leaking from our tongues
Yet your shy legs crossed anxious
        Concealing your most precious parts
In a flash we were already getting down to it
And it's hard to forget
        That first time you opened up to me
        Gushing with the thought of me
The way you dreamed of this moment
The way I dreamed of this moment
I was as close to you as I'll ever be
Do you remember it like I do?
How could you forget.

**Keys To Your Car**

And you actually believe that I
      Caused your last relationship to fail
To think so little of me
Suppressing how much you wanted it too.

*It's easy to blame others for your own mistakes.*

**Untitled I**

And with all the tears I've cried for you
I hope to drown myself
       Out of existence.

## The Weight On Our Shoulders

I wish I knew what happened to my beloved
You're not her
You're not even a cheap knockoff
You're cold and full of deception
But Lord knows
     If I knew my baby was out there
I'd go to the ends of the earth
     To find her once again.

**Car Wash**

I remember those nights
The late night drives
We could talk about anything
         And it was enough
We were mirror images
         Bonding over the smallest details
And I can't help but think about what you said
         One night
         How you told me
                  *You really made me fall for you…*
God, that was the greatest feeling
How much impact those words held to me
It melted my heart away
         Too bad, it was just another lie.

**Untitled II**

Do you still reach for me now that I've gone?
     I still reach for you.

## Dressing Rooms

Crossing paths once more
      While I still have this love for you…
It's unfair
It's fucked up
Because I know when you see me
You feel nothing at all
And I'm left with the weight of this world.

**Sunday Brunch**

If only I could go back to that coffee shop with you
One more time
Nothing was more perfect.

## Can I Ask You A Personal Question?

How much easier it must have been
To send that message
Than look me in the face and say it
Knowing damn well you couldn't
I mean
        I was there when he wasn't
        And I know you only left me for him.

**The Pickup Lines**

With all the people on this earth
I choose you
And if that doesn't mean anything to you
        I don't know what does.

## Our Concerts

Sometimes we'd just sit in the car
And play music

I don't think I'll ever find something more intimate
	Than those moments with you.

## Official Dates

Oh how badly I want you to think of me
     And how I know you never do
Because you never cared about me
     The way I cared about you
I was just there to take his place
     A substitute if you will
And on his return I became nothing
So shut me out while you still can
Tell me it was only fake feelings
Push me to that edge once again
So this time
I can finally take care of some unfinished business
With a single pull
     Of the trigger.

## St. Louis No. 2

Sometimes I keep myself up at night
Sometimes I listen to sad songs
        Or songs that remind me of you
Sometimes I make myself cry
        Just to make the pain stay
And one way or another it stays
And it carves into my heart
Sometimes I do this
        Maybe with a pen or rather a blade
I do this
Just to know it was real
Just to know that I can still feel something.

**Untitled III**

I hope who ever finds you next
    Is more prepared to lose you
        Than I was.

## Big Dipper

I told you before we made those moves
    Once we cross this bridge
    We could never return to being
    *Just friends*
And that will always hold true
So don't come back to me
    Pretending like all you ever wanted
    Was me and you playing house
        But only ever living as friends.

## Will I See You Tomorrow?

When you look back do you see it?
How awful you've become
How far from yourself you are now
Amazing, how quickly you became a stranger
    To the girl I fell in love with

How different you were back then
    Full of love, smiles, and hope
What happened to that beautiful young woman
    My best friend
        The one I'd do anything on this earth
        To save.

## Untitled IV

And with a single breath
    She vanished from my life.

## Baggage Claim

How many lies did you tell yourself
How long did you go
     Knowing deep down
          You could never love me
Forever feeling remorse
     For becoming
          A little more than friendly
My thoughts; you really wanted me
     Well that's what you said isn't it
But I guess that too
     Was another great lie of yours
You ended up dealing with the issue
You confronted those feelings
Now I'm nothing to you
     Like I always was or will be
But tell me this
     How long do you expect to go
          Before telling him the truth.

**A Song To Show Me**

Every song I hear reminds me of you
How you'd sing ever so beautifully
This music we shared
          You loved what I loved
And now the radio is full of your voice
So on my knees I pray to God for silence.

## This Bouquet, You Never Received

I hate that I know you
All of you
    The superficial
        The intimate
            Damn near everything
I hate that you threw it all away
    For no reason at all…

## Untitled V

The miles chewed you up
    And spat you out.

## Missing Persons

A picture of us from the past
     Caused me so much hurt
Not because I miss you
Not because I love you
Not because we seemed so happy
No
Because the girl in the picture
     She was almost unrecognized
She passed away what seems like
     A lifetime ago.

## Drowning Demons

The rain calls out your name
      With every single drop
The sky is crying for you, you know
      The Earth knows what She lost.

**I've Waited Here For You**

This world without you
      It seems so meaningless
Eyes frosted with bloodied tears
      Blinds me from moving on
Seeing only this moment
Forever living this life without you.

*It's called Everlong...*

## Untitled VI

And how quickly
    It withers
        Away...

## Cookie Dough

And how you play it off
Like you never even met me
How we never happened
As if I was never a part of your life
     When it was me in the spotlight
That pains me the most
That you're lying to yourself
     To your friends
          To your family
And you're lying to me
     The one you used to call your best friend
     Your closeted lover
     The one who'd do anything for you
And you might try to erase me
     Forget me
Or whatever the hell you do
     To get past the thought of me
But I'll never forget you
Especially how you treated me
     In the end.

## Chocolate And Strawberry Please

You mean a lot to me
>    *You mean a lot to me too*
I care about you
>    *I care about you too*
I miss you so much
>    *I miss you so much too*
I love you.

>    You mean a lot to me
>    >    *I know*
>    I care about you too
>    >    *I know*
>    I miss you so much
>    >    *Yeah*
>    I love you
>    >    *I know.*

>    >    You mean the world to me
>    >    I care about you so much
>    >    I can't wait to see you
>    >    You know I love you
>    >    >    *You know I never did.*

**And Ryo Finally Reveals Himself**

I want you back so bad
So bad, you can't even imagine that
And you don't even think about us
      What I'd do for you
      How much I loved you
You've thrown away our past
      Full of happiness
And there's nothing you want to do to fix this
I can't understand
      Begin to imagine why
With you everything seemed so perfect
So tell me why you lied
This heartache stings
      *IT'S KILLED ME*
I loved you forever
      But you just let me die
        And die
          And die
So I no longer sleep
I stay up, tears flooding my floor
      Tears of a better life
        Memories so beautiful in shape
You poisoned me with loss
Left untreated and alone
      I can't quite see it
        How you got so cold.

**Still Watching?**

He will never love you as much as I have
And I would rather die
      Knowing that as fact
Than continue living in this lie.

**Untitled VII**

You became the one thing
You swore to never become
A manipulator
  A liar
    A fake
      A cheat
        But more importantly
        My traitor.

## The Tragedy Of Secret Lovers

I guess it's poetic
Because I know how he must have felt
When you went from him to me
            In a matter of seconds
I know…
You did the same thing to me
You broke my heart and moved on to a new victim
So yeah I know how he must have felt
In fact
I know how he feels to this day
Because I still think of you every now and then
            I'm sure he does too
                    But you
                        No
You don't remember at all do you?
You wipe your memory clean
            Just to do it all over again
So if you're anything
            Like I know you are,
I pray for your new host
And certainly the one that follows.

**In Your Room // Braces**

Waking up to your girl
    Who is no longer interested in you
        Prompted by nothing
        No trouble
        No fights
Has its own suspicions attached
    And even in my darkest hours
I told you we could work it out,
*I don't want to try again right now…*
    *Or anytime soon.*

## The Skylift, That's My Favorite

Like air you are free
Leaving my body behind
Slipped away; breathless.

**Christmas Lights In The Park**

And I guess you were just as bad
    As those ex's you talked about
I learned that the hard way when I realized
    I couldn't trust you in the slightest.

## Obsession // Self-harm

Rain falls over head
Reminding me not to leave my bed
And everyday I wake to pain
Forever aching since you came.

## Half Shell

I can't stand to see myself
  Back at me, a failure
I failed to keep you happy
I failed to keep you here
And when you stare at yourself long enough
  You know you're different
  You're changed
  Empty
And there's nothing you can do to fill that
  That hole in your heart
It's as if I'm half the man I used to be
And my other half has just walked away
So I continue to stare at this mirror
  Begging to be released from this
  Begging to be dead.

## I Never Felt It Back

You made me believe it was so real
      When really,
I was never anything more
      Than convenience to you.

**They Hurt You The Most // Pretty Good Lot**

I left you before
      Back then
And you called out my name again
You were broken
And my heart still beat for you
      So I came back
          I healed your aching heart
I sewed up your wounds
But you payed me back with abuse
      You tore my heart out
      You shattered me to dust
      You were merciless
And I know that you have no intentions
      Of resurrecting me
          The way I did to you.

**Good Morning Beautiful**

How hard it is
Waking up in a bed without you
While you spend your nights with him.

## PTC Paper

You're not wide awake at night
Thinking of reaching out to me
      With tears rolling down your cheeks
           No
And that's the reason I'm wide awake at night
Reaching for the blade
Allowing these drops of red to *slide* down my bed
      Effortlessly
Because I know you
      I know you would never try for me
           You don't even try for yourself.

## Big Hearts // Slave Away

Seeing nothing but the good in someone
Who never saw a damn thing in you
        Is the worst.

**They Already Think We Are**

You were my number one
        My partner
And we spent every second
        Of every goddamn day together
So how the fuck am I supposed to go on
        Without you.

## The Bill

How used
How manipulated
Letting me in to strike at the heart of another
Sacrificing my life
     For the sake of your own
And I believed it too
Thought we were real
     And I loved you so so much
I was sure of that,
But under that thick smile
     Under those thick lies
You never felt anything like you said you did
You never wanted me like you said you did
What you wanted was company
     To help you get through the days
     To not feel that feeling, loneliness
You were alone, so you found me
     To make you happy when he couldn't
     To help you when he couldn't
     To listen to you when he wouldn't
I was there
I was always there
And dammit I fell so hard for you
     It worked, all the lies of wanting me
And now what
You found your way back into his arms

60

After all we did behind his back
E R A S E D
After all we shared
E R A S E D
After how we loved
E R A S E D
And to go from love to hate so quickly
In an instant
Without any warning
Must be the work of him.

**Win Me A Prize // Cranes**

I wish you'd escape my mind
As fast as I escaped your heart.

## FaceTimed Out

She looks so sweet when you find her
But she's a bad, bad girl
You wanna believe she's pure
      But she's the furthest thing from it
So please, don't make the mistake of thinking
      She would change her ways for you.

**And You Don't Even Look Anymore**

I first saw you
And I never thought you'd be a part of my life,
Was I lucky to have been so wrong
Or was having you nothing but a curse.

**Can I Have A Hug?**

I let myself trust you
    That was my biggest mistake
I thought we were lock and key
    But you tore us to shreds
        Making confetti out of my love
And as I hit the floor my mind went numb
    You never gave me a chance
        To imagine a life without you.

## NDE

The sky cries
And I can't help but miss you in the storm
Hoping the tears will wash away
     All my memories of you.

**The New Cancer**

I was unpacking my belongings when it hit
The gradual slowdown of movements
        As I stared at the chipped white wall ahead
I held back that urge to cry
        But it stung like a motherfucker
Knowing I'd lost you for good
Knowing I have found myself
        Crawling back into bed with Loneliness
The only one who accepts me for me
The only one I'm burdened to live with

Although I choose to love you instead...

**Python II**

A perfect machine is not put out of working order
Without the interference
    Of another variable.

**Throat Of The World**

Molten ember lust blanketed the cobalt sky
Surrounded by our celestial bodies shining bright
    In desire
It was like making love
      Being in each other's presence as we danced
          To the moonlight symphony
But earth continued it's rotation on us
And rotations lead to spins
And spins to distance
And your flare began to fade with time
In a fiery explosion you erupted
      Dissolving into stardust
      Leaving the sky empty
      Leaving my heart voided
Tears stained the starlight dance floor
*Who would share this moonlight with me?*
So I too froze myself, dying out in a vacant light
And all along the suns
      And the cosmos
          Constantly sought your return
And all along the suns
      And the cosmos
          Constantly seek your return.

## And You Love This Kind Of Shit

I've been entombed in a coffin of loss
I count my breaths in hopes
    Of your saving grace once more
*Though I know you'll have me buried in it.*

**Green Jacket**

Seal my eyes
     Lock my heart
For I never want to feel this love again
It was the strongest I'd ever felt
     So real
          Yet to you so fake
The heartbreak after was enough to kill me...

So I let it.

**Ants From Up Here**

How long can I go
Distracting my mind from you
Before groveling to the gods
For your return.

**April Showers**

It's 2:39 in the morning
        When I record the time of death
I should be asleep
        But She is keeping me up in my head
Our room, so cold and close
We watch together
        The last petal fade from Her
And all the while the final grain
Falls from the hourglass making a seemingly
        Earth shattering *clunk* as it hits the bottom
She just wanted to be called Lily
        But everyone knew She'd be better off
                As Bloodroot.


*-I think if I had a back up I'd own like a greenhouse, you
know with flowers and stuff.*
*-Do you remember myyyy favorite flower??*
*-Of course I do...*

## Untitled VIII

I was building you a monument
While you were digging me a grave.

**Gamora**

The fire in our love, born from the dark
Behind the back of an unsuspecting one
Birthed from under the covers
But when the last love left you
I moved up to take his place
The fire in our love grew dim to your taste
What seemed like love to one
Was only company to the other
We died from under the covers
When you strangled your former lover.

**Floral Sundress // Pink Skies**

And evermore the sun and the moon
    Will still make love to your beautiful skin
Not realizing how lucky they truly are.

**Sweethearts <3**

And somewhere out there I know
You're making drunken love to a man
Who only cares about you when he's not sober.

## Cinderella

Every morning I'm sick
Feeling ill and insanely tired
My first thoughts are of you
Probably from that nightmare
        I just so happened to wake up from
And it kills my mood and will to live
So I lie here in bed for an hour or two
Thinking of all the ways I used to love you
It only hurts me more
        Confuses me more
                I can't understand it
Why you left me so damaged
        The way you just disappeared
What did I do to see this side of you?

And when I finally get up to sob in the shower
I dream of all the ways to get you back
        I drown away the pain
                I sit alone in silence

Wet, shivering, debating whether or not
        To reach out to you
        Knowing damn well it'll never be the same
        Knowing you'd be angry with me
        Knowing you'd be annoyed
But not truly understanding how or why
        These feelings came to be

I really thought you wanted me
I really thought you cared
And for a moment,
      I even thought you might have loved me too.

**Painting You**

You opened me up to a world
I was never ready to be a part of.

**It's Not The Same**

Our hearts erupted
And I thought they'd never burn out
What a shame,
      I was so wrong.

## Lies // Love // Longing

Maybe I hate you
You cheated and lied me to death
A pretender who acted like everything was perfect
Although you couldn't shake the hold
  He put you in

And you came with baggage
  An ex was still on your mind
In fact the only time he wasn't there
  Was when my hands were all over you
  Pleasing you when he couldn't
But it wasn't the same I suppose
  Because you made distance
And when you had your chance to run you took it
You found yourself back at his place, I'm sure
Fucking him without remorse for the lonely heart
  You left back home, me
The one who truly loved you
The one you truly cheated on.

## Untitled IX

Just as the stars in the night sky
She is all too visible
And all too far away.

**A Dream About You**

In my dreams we're always so happy
Then I wake up,
    Breakdown in the bathroom
Where my only company comes
    From the lost soul in the mirror.

**Homewrecker**

Do you want me to sing you to sleep
    In this violet city
        This underground
Where all the neon lights
        Have blinded us from the black alone
*We will no longer let you manipulate us*
We rise up
        With pistols in our heads
            And beliefs on our arms
These firearms fight back the monster in your heart
The one that left me here
        On our sacrificial honeymoon
So with sin out of the way,
        Are we even fucking lovers
Or just tourists to rock bottom
        Where the darkest nights
        Shine just as bright as the purest hearts
        And the purest hearts are nothing short
            Of sinister
What losers we are
To have believed this was so right
When every night with you
        Was so wrong.

## He's Not Always Bad

You could either be popping pills
    Or relieving the blood from your arms
And whichever you choose
You know it'd be better than facing the truth
You're so scared of it
    It makes you look weak
You won't even take a glimpse
    At how broken
        You really are.

**Once A Liar**

You promised to tell me everything
That we would hold no secrets
And yet you hid this behind my back.

**White Converse**

Thank you for taking it all from me
And leaving me with *black*
That rigid splintered mood cutting into...
    And my hearing had gone *black*
        STATIC DEAFNESS PAUSED
With the love on my tongue still *black*
Never to shake your taste in everyone everywhere
    And I try to hide from you
But I know my life will always be *black*.

## No Such Thing As 'Wrong Timing'

For your sake I hope the memory of us dissolves
That you never think of me again
You never wonder what if
You never whisper my name
Cause I know that's what you'd want
     To believe we never met
     Believe we never made love
     Believe we never burned out
As for me
I hope to never love again
Never open myself up to this horror
     Denying all friendships
Because you took my heart and robbed me
     Of everything I was willing to give
And in the rain you'll find me
     After all the times we shared
          Cursing to the heavens;
*Fuck you for breaking me down*
     *Fuck this world that our paths ever crossed.*

**Tatted // Pierced**

You did it once before
      Did you do it again?
      Did it seem right?
      Did it seem fair?
Did loving him behind my back
      Remind you of our own
        Forbidden fire.

## Are You Okay?

She leaves the crime scene without a scratch
A trail of blood stains the concrete floor
Her withered grey eyes are anything but innocent
But her pearly lace dress stays pure
The man she left- forgotten
  A lover of the past
The one who'd give his dying breath for her
  Has traded in his last

With a stunning 231 stab wounds
He has surely passed away
  A hole for every compliment
  A hole for every day
  A hole for all the times he said *I love you*
  Or every time he begged you *stay*
  A hole for all the fun they had
  A hole for all the hours
  And every time they went to Comics
    To talk about superpowers

And in his final moments
He still whispered to her love
One last puncture finally sent him above
Now the killer in this plot
  Well she's too sly to catch
No one on planet earth
  Could have, would have guessed
She made him believe in love

Made others believe it too
But that's what makes a brilliant killer
The twisted side of you.

**Infamous Snap**

Months later
I'm still plagued by your smile
　　Where did you go…
　　　　My little one.

**Over Our Summer**

You pretend to be pure hearted
You pretend that you miss me
     But you refuse my calls
Claim you're 'too tired'
     'Too busy'
That's why I know
     If I really needed you
          I can find you sleeping with your ex.

**WW**

Let it be known
    That if our eyes shall ever meet again
    I will not have the strength
        To hold back the loss
           So much loss
You'll be able to read it on my face
And by the time you look away
Our whole life from birth to chaos
    Will have flashed before those eyes
        Breaking your heart
Just as you have broke mine.

## Hopefully Eternally

Nowadays I can't even find the time to sleep
I'm too busy spending nights
    Waiting for your return
    Waiting on that text
        I'm certain you'll never send
All the while aching from the pit in my heart
And just praying for some rest.

**Left Handed Driver**

How quickly you became my enemy
    After countless nights of wishing
    You were more than just a friend,
That is the great tragedy in young love.

## Will You Still Visit Me?

How hard my life has become
How much more complicated
How one person can manipulate my world
    I can't escape you
    I can't escape you in anything
You've left your mark on me
Now I have to find a way to live with it.

**The Current**

While you've moved backwards
Just to have your heart broken as before
I've learned to never trust anyone ever again.

**Do You Really Want Me Making A Decision At
Two In The Morning???**

When we talked for the last time
I never really believed it was you
      Cold, direct, unaffectionate
That couldn't have been you...

Or maybe that was the only time
      You ever chose to show your real self.

## Unfriended

It's so hard to understand
I was always there for you
     No matter what
But in a moment of weakness
You wouldn't even listen to me
     And I tried to fix us
     I would have done anything
But you were hellbent on leaving me to die

And I'll never forgive you for that.

**Bunny**

All I ask
Is that you feel the pain you've dealt me
    I hope you fall in love
    I hope you're happy
    And most of all
    I hope it comes crashing down before you
Then
    Maybe
You'll know what it feels like
    And better yet
        Maybe
            You'll know regret.

## Ever Be Friends Again?

For the longest time it was difficult without you
I couldn't think of anything I had to hate
I couldn't think of anything that was wrong
But I guess that's what I hate
That nothing was ever wrong
You just gave up
      And so I thought
      And thought
      And thought
And I realized how much he still meant to you
You see I know you better than you think
I know the guilt of cheating
      It must have killed you…
It killed us

You felt like you didn't deserve me
That it wasn't right after what we did
And that's shitty
You lied to him
And you used me
You threw me away when you couldn't take it
How selfish
      How immature
Every decision you made was wrong
      And you're still so fucking wrong
Because you tried to have it all
And baby, I told you from the beginning
      *You can never have both.*

## DDT

Whether you knew it or not
I always understood your depression
And I would've done anything on this earth
     To help you conquer it
But I guess you just found it easier
     To give it all away.

**One More Lap**

You left me for dead
But you underestimate my resolve
I will come back from this stronger
        Better than before
And one day I'm sure you'll regret this.

**Bus Ride**

I felt like I knew you all my life
And then you lied to me...
You told me you wanted me forever
But every morning I awake in awe, alone
Seeing that I have survived
      Another day without you
      Another day without my better half
      Another day wishing to break this silence.

**Triple Word Score**

The thought of you tortures me
When it used to bring me peace of mind
How I wish it still did
      More than anything
And I know
      It still should.

## Bleed Me Dry

To be apart from you
Is to be torn from you
And to let you go
Is to be taken from you
And as I wait
Across this world for you
Know I am thinking
Of ways to get to you
And every night
I'll say goodnight to you
Through the distance
May not seem right to you
Just know no bounds
Will keep my heart from you
This guarantee
I'm always part of you.

**Would You Like To Read It?**

And how difficult it is to write about you this way
When all I ever did was love you
From that very first moment.

*I finally got around to writing that book about you.*

**Untitled X**

You can still find me at our favorite spot
Wishing upon the midnight sky
For the day
When our timing will finally be right.

## And The Eyes Were Our Thing

Eyeshadow of oceans and evergreen
Finally fade from face
Needles from your grey pines fall
      Pikes and lances to pin me down
I beg for your release
I beg to be saved by you once more.

**More Than Anything**

Sometimes I find myself still writing about you
Just to see if I remember how much
     I really loved you.

## August

And maybe one day
We'll get the chance to do it right
Maybe one day
We'll lock eyes in the pouring rain
Reliving the union of two lost souls
Becoming intertwined like we first met
And maybe just maybe one day
You'll walk up to me in that beautiful storm
      And say;
        *You're still the one with all the love to give.*

## The One I'm Waiting On // Don't Wait For Me

I've made a lot of sacrifices for you and yet
I would do them all again to get you back
And I'm sure you believe that.

**Barefoot On The Grass**

And after everything
You're still you
And I still love you
That may be the worst part of it all.

## A Level Beyond

Maybe one day these will reach you
And I hope you remember all that I was
Doing whatever I could to make you happy
Even if it took everything
          Especially if it took everything
Because unlike you, I did feel something
Something so powerful
          That to say you didn't feel it too
Is nothing but you lying to yourself.

**Blueberry Muffins**

And in those moments
You were lacking what it meant to be truly loved
So at least now you understand
What to look for in friends
      Family
            Lovers
Now you know who to be
And with that,
I believe I was meant to be in your life
Even if
      We were only ever young lovers.

## Our Quiet Place

This pain you traded me for my love
It burns like a fire inside
All the ways I showed you my heart
    Meaningless to you now
The lengths I went to make you mine
The lengths I went to please you
    Christmas, birthdays, Valentines
Bloodshot eyes and swollen lids
    From tears that sever layers of skin
All the ways I showed you my heart
Anything I'd do to love you…
…And after it all there wasn't even a moment
    A sliver of a second you ever felt it back
No matter what I did or didn't do
So I lie here,
A stream of drops from the shower head hit me
And as I pick up the knife
You collect your razors too
And we *cut* and *sever* and *slice*
Miles apart, hearts now torn apart
    Houses alone
We *cut* and *cut* and *cut*
And for a second,
    I feel I share one last moment with you.

Also check out these books by the same author:

**Quadrantaria.**

**Ice Cream And Suicide**

Made in the USA
San Bernardino, CA
08 December 2019